A Life Like No Other

Jesus.

In three and a half years, a Jewish carpenter from the backwater town of Nazareth in the backwater Roman province of Galilee lived a life so extraordinary it transformed the world. Though He wrote no books and built no edifices, countless books have been written about Him, and churches and cathedrals honoring Him have been erected all over the world.

Jesus was born to humble parents in an obscure animal pen. He ministered, not in the garden spot of the world or in palatial temples, but in the insignificant sun-baked land of Israel among the desperate and the destitute. And yet, all who came before or after Him—in all their power and prestige—compared to Jesus, were but lint upon the pages of history.

Only one name continues to fascinate and capture the imagination of all humanity. And only one name continues to divide and to unify it: Jesus.

When Jesus ministered on earth, He said to His disciples: "Do not think that I came to bring peace on the earth; I did not come to bring peace, but a sword. For I came to set a man against his father, and a daughter against her mother, and a daughter-in-law against her mother-in-law; and a man's enemies will be the members of his household" (Matthew 10:34–36). During Christ's earthly ministry, He was a dividing line, a *scandalon* or "stumbling block" (1 Corinthians 1:23), to the Jews who rejected His teaching and His offer of the kingdom. He remains scandalous to this day.

At the same time, no person has united peoples from different races, creeds, and economic conditions as Jesus has. People from every tribe, tongue, and nation find in Jesus the very source of truth, meaning, and life eternal.

Who but Jesus could divide the world as He does? Who but Jesus could unite the world as He does? Who but Jesus possesses a "name which is above every name, so that at the name of Jesus every knee will bow, of those who are in heaven and on earth and under the earth, and that every tongue will confess that Jesus Christ is Lord" (Philippians 2:9–11)?

No one, living or dead, has transformed the human heart and mind or changed the course of history as Jesus has. How could He accomplish what so many before and since have failed to accomplish? The answer is both simple and profound: from AD 29 to AD 33, Jesus demonstrated to a watching world what it was like for God to walk the earth.

The book you hold in your hands is the third and final in Insight for Living Ministries' trilogy on the birth, ministry, and passion of Jesus Christ. *Three Years with Jesus: A Pictorial Journey Through the Ministry of Christ* takes a chronological look at some of the most significant events in Jesus's ministry. Each devotional will remind you once again of the remarkable life of our Savior and Lord. My hope is that it will cause you to fall on your knees in worship and praise.

Bowing with you,

Chuck

Charles R. Swindoll

Mount of Beatitudes

Capernaum

Bethsaida

Sower's Cove

Tabgha

Sea of Galilee shoreline from abov

Table of Contents

A LIFE LIKE NO OTHER 1

KEY PLACES IN JESUS'S GALILEE MINISTRY 2

PREPARATIONS 4
4 BC TO AD 29

THE EARLY MONTHS OF MINISTRY 10
FALL OF AD 29 TO SPRING OF AD 30

A YEAR OF POPULARITY 20
PASSOVER OF AD 30 TO PASSOVER OF AD 31

A YEAR OF TRANSITION 30
PASSOVER OF AD 31 TO PASSOVER OF AD 32

THE FINAL YEAR: LOOKING AHEAD TO JERUSALEM 42
PASSOVER OF AD 32 TO PASSOVER OF AD 33

APPENDIX: OUTLINE OF CHRIST'S MINISTRY 60

HOW TO BEGIN A RELATIONSHIP WITH GOD 62

WE ARE HERE FOR YOU 64

ORDERING INFORMATION 64

QUESTIONS FOR FAMILY TALKS AND GROUP DISCUSSIONS 66

ENDNOTES 71

Preparations . . .

4 BC to AD 29

Modern-day Nazareth

HE REMAINED [IN EGYPT] UNTIL THE DEATH OF HEROD.
This was to fulfill WHAT HAD BEEN SPOKEN BY THE LORD THROUGH
THE PROPHET: "OUT OF EGYPT I CALLED *My Son.*"

—MATTHEW 2:15

G OD HAD KEPT *His* PROMISE. Jesus was born . . . King of the Jews.

But King Herod the Great could not tolerate a rival to his throne, so he ordered all Bethlehem boys killed who were 2 years old and under. To avoid the slaughter, Joseph and Mary and Jesus escaped to Egypt and remained there until Herod died. According to the apostle Matthew, all of these events had a purpose in the sovereign plan of God (Matthew 2:15).

Then, as if retracing the steps of the Exodus, Jesus's family left Egypt for the land that God had promised to Israel so long ago. Throughout their history, God's people had chosen to worship false gods and so suffered repeated invasions by enemy nations until finally they were exiled from the Promised Land. When restored to their home, they worshiped God outwardly while worshiping wealth in their hearts. To judge that sin, God withdrew His protection, gave them over to corrupt leaders, and stopped speaking to them. By the time of King Herod four hundred years later, the religious leaders of Israel had erected a new idol to stand alongside that of wealth: their own self-righteousness.

It was during His people's centuries-long period of wandering from God that the boy Jesus came to Israel. As Joseph and Mary reentered the Promised Land, perhaps only weeks after leaving, they discovered that Jesus's throne was still occupied. Herod the Great was dead, but his son Archelaus, a man even more brutal and erratic than his father, reigned in Herod's place. So the two young parents set aside their expectation that their Messiah would reign anytime soon and returned to their home in the forgotten little town of Nazareth. Sometime during the eleven years that followed, the memories of their adventure in Bethlehem faded, washed out by the humdrum of daily existence.

Jesus was a boy with a destiny, and His destiny would affect everyone He touched.[1]

See Matthew 2.

By the time Joseph, Mary, and Jesus entered Egypt, the Great Sphinx of Giza had been standing for more than 2,000 years.

As part of God's providential preparation, Egypt had a Jewish population of approximately one million. The area was out of Herod's jurisdiction, so it offered an ideal place for escape. Matthew compared Jesus's leaving Egypt with the Exodus, making history—in this instance—prophetic (Matthew 2:15). Ironically, both the nation of Israel as well as Jesus went down to Egypt under the leadership of a man named Joseph who had dreams from God.

Model of the temple as it looked in the first century

HE SAID TO THEM, "WHY IS IT THAT YOU WERE *looking for Me?* DID YOU NOT KNOW THAT I HAD TO BE IN *My Father's* HOUSE?"

—LUKE 2:49

AT AGE 13, A JEWISH BOY WAS CALLED A *bar mitzvah*, a "son of the commandment." In preparation for His thirteenth birthday, Jesus might have undergone a rigorous program of instruction and training for this passage into manhood. Regardless, one year prior to officially becoming a man, Jesus accompanied His family's caravan to the Holy City to celebrate the Passover Feast and the Feast of Unleavened Bread.

After the celebration came to a close, Joseph and Mary began the journey north to Galilee along with hundreds of other pilgrims, including dozens of friends and extended relatives. Perhaps thinking Jesus had joined His cousins farther back, the couple discovered only later that Jesus was not in their number

On most Mondays and Thursdays, you can still find at least one bar mitzvah *celebration occurring at Jerusalem's Western Wall.*

at all. Immediately, Joseph and Mary turned again for Jerusalem and retraced their steps. After three days of searching, they finally found Jesus in the temple, surrounded by the nation's foremost experts in Jewish Law.

As Joseph and Mary entered the scene, they were dumbstruck to find their son in the temple. They had probably worried that He was dead in a gutter. (That's usually the place a parent's mind goes when a child can't be found.) So, naturally, they spoke to Jesus like any parent would upon finding a lost child.

Jesus was genuinely confused by their searching for three days before looking in the temple. If they had remembered His beginnings or recalled the words of Simeon, the temple would have been their first place to look upon returning to Jerusalem. Where else would the Son of God be but in the house of God? Nevertheless, Joseph and Mary didn't connect the dots. "They did not understand the statement which He had made to them" (Luke 2:50).

The irony of this episode is absolutely priceless. Joseph and Mary — firsthand witnesses to angelic announcements of Jesus's coming, the shepherds' and magi's worship of the child Jesus, and prophetic oracles — didn't have the eyes to see Jesus's divine purpose emerging. Jesus, however, knew what was happening to Himself. He understood His purpose, His call, His divinely appointed mission.

Tragically, most people don't discover their purpose until late in life. Some never find it.[2]

See Luke 2:41–52.

The religious leaders' response to the boy Jesus could be paraphrased, "They were beside themselves" (Luke 2:47). Jesus was able to put things together and come up with insights that should have been far beyond His grasp at age 12. He could go to the heart of an issue like no one they had ever seen.

The Early Months of Ministry . . .

Fall of AD 29 to Spring of AD 30

Synagogue in Capernaum

The Jordan River, traditionally the location of Jesus's baptism

AFTER BEING BAPTIZED, *Jesus came up* IMMEDIATELY FROM THE

WATER; AND BEHOLD, THE HEAVENS WERE OPENED, AND

[JOHN THE BAPTIZER] SAW THE *Spirit of God descending*

AS A DOVE AND LIGHTING ON HIM.

— MATTHEW 3:16

Baptism— A Symbolic Doorway

N UMEROUS PEOPLE CLAIMED TO BE THE *Christ* in first-century Israel. But John, known as "the Baptizer," didn't claim to be the Messiah—only the forerunner, sent by God to prepare the people for the promised King's appearance.

John called Israel to repentance and administered the traditional Jewish rite of baptism, whereby converts to Judaism were ceremonially cleansed as they became, as it were, adopted sons of the covenant. John's baptism of repentance called Jews to admit they had forsaken their covenant with God and to approach Him as if for the very first time. By submitting to John's baptism, they were essentially starting over with God.

The rite of baptism had another meaning that would be important to Jesus. Baptism was the rite of priests who were purified by the washing of water just prior to representing the people before God in the Most Holy Place.

In AD 29, eighteen to twenty years after Jesus became a son of the covenant, He presented Himself to John for baptism. At first, John refused, saying, "I have need to be baptized by You, and do You come to me?" (Matthew 3:14). John mistakenly thought Jesus was submitting Himself to the prophet's baptism of repentance, but Jesus had something else in mind. He was about to give the symbol of immersion in water a new meaning and change the rite of baptism forever.

Jesus entered the waters of the Jordan River to be immersed and, with a host of John's disciples and other witnesses looking on, welcomed the affirmation of His Father. As the Spirit of God appeared as a dove descending upon Jesus, a booming voice shook the crowd: "This is My beloved Son, in whom I am well-pleased" (3:17).

That day, Jesus officially began a journey that would lead to His ultimate destiny. His ritual cleansing publicly announced the beginning of His ministry—the pursuit of His call. And His first act was to make baptism a symbolic doorway to a new kind of life, through which He would be the first to walk.[1]

See Matthew 3.

Ritual baths by the Southern Steps of the Temple Mount. Ancient oral commentaries on the Old Testament required that Jews be ritually pure upon entering the Temple Mount. In most cases, purification could be achieved by bathing in rainwater collected in a ritual bath called a mikveh. Immersion was not a new practice, but when John and Jesus came along, they gave this familiar rite new meaning.

Outside the Bible, the word baptizo was used in reference to a piece of fabric that was placed into dye. Hence, the term came to have a figurative meaning: whatever was "baptized into" something was identified with it (Romans 6:3; 1 Corinthians 10:2; 12:13; Galatians 3:27).

The Judean Wilderness, near the location where Jesus was tempted

THEN *Jesus was led up* BY THE SPIRIT INTO
THE WILDERNESS TO BE *tempted* BY THE DEVIL.

— MATTHEW 4:1

Before officially *beginning His* public ministry, Jesus departed for the Judean Wilderness for an extended period of solitude and fasting. Matthew states that the Holy Spirit led Jesus there specifically "to be tempted by the devil" (Matthew 4:1).

After Jesus had spent forty days with only water to drink, Satan confronted Him with a proposition: "If You are the Son of God, tell this stone to become bread" (Luke 4:3). On the surface, it was a reasonable suggestion. But Jesus came to earth to be the man all other men failed to be and to become the king Israel had always needed—a king who would depend upon God completely and serve Him consistently. The response of Jesus to this temptation recalls the words of Moses to the Israelites in the desert: "Man shall not live on bread alone, but on every word that proceeds out of the mouth of God" (Matthew 4:4; see also Deuteronomy 8:3).

As he continued his attack on the integrity of the Messiah, Satan transported Jesus to the pinnacle of the Jewish temple in Jerusalem, either literally or in a vision, and challenged Him to leap to the crowded street below. Satan cleverly twisted Psalm 91:11–12 to imply that the Jews would immediately recognize the miracle and accept Jesus as the Messiah. Again He responded with a quotation from the Old Testament. He recalled the words of Moses to the Israelites, who refused to believe in God's protection without a miraculous sign: "You shall not put the Lord your God to the test" (Matthew 4:7).

God's promise that this new kingdom would encompass the entire world became the focus of Satan's third and final attempt to corrupt Jesus during His time in the desert. Having shown Jesus the splendor of all the world's kingdoms, Satan said, "All these things I will give You, if You fall down and worship me" (4:9). Jesus again responded with a quotation from the Old Testament, "Go, Satan! For it is written, 'You shall worship the Lord your God and serve Him only'" (4:10).

In time, Jesus would indeed go to Jerusalem to present Himself in the temple as the Messiah, but not before proving Himself to be a king worthy of Israel's throne.[2]

See Matthew 4:1–11.

The southwest corner of the Temple Mount in Jerusalem could have represented the "pinnacle" of the temple in Jesus's day. It was at this corner that the priests would stand and blow the shofar horn, announcing the beginning of Sabbaths and holy days. The street below would have been filled with people on any given day. The excavated street is still visible today.

Hebrew text of Deuteronomy 8. When He was tempted by Satan, Jesus quoted memorized verses exclusively from the book of Deuteronomy.

"Bethany Beyond the Jordan" stood as an ideal locale for John the Baptizer's ministry — as well as for Jesus to begin His ministry. This area across from Jericho served historically as the place where the mantle was passed from Moses to Joshua, then from Elijah to Elisha, and finally, from John to Jesus. This place represented new beginnings for Israel

HE FOUND FIRST HIS OWN BROTHER *Simon* AND SAID TO HIM,

"WE HAVE FOUND *the Messiah*" (WHICH TRANSLATED MEANS CHRIST).

— JOHN 1:41

Two of John the Baptizer's *disciples*— Andrew and John, the son of Zebedee—upon hearing the forerunner call Jesus "the Lamb of God," left to follow Jesus home (John 1:35–37). Imagine the conversation that took place that afternoon and evening as Andrew and John listened to Jesus's dinner talk. It obviously had a profound impact on Andrew, who left early the next morning to find his brother and bring him to meet the rabbi.

> One of the two who heard John speak and followed Him, was Andrew, Simon Peter's brother. He found first his own brother Simon and said to him, "We have found the Messiah" (which translated means Christ). He brought him to Jesus. Jesus looked at him and said, "You are Simon the son of John; you shall be called Cephas" (which is translated Peter). (1:40–42)

Cephas derives from an Aramaic word meaning "rock." Simon was a fisherman by trade and powerfully built after years of throwing nets and hauling up loads of fish. The winsome rabbi, Jesus, probably put a hand on Simon's shoulder while greeting him and decided the nickname "Rocky" or "Rock-man" was fitting. (Of course, Jesus intended a double meaning, which would only become clear later.) And so the name stuck: Cephas—*Petros* to the Greeks, Peter in English.

As the small group of men enjoyed the presence and words of Jesus, Peter began to realize that Andrew was right. The men had found the Messiah and very much wanted to become His disciples. But discipleship in the first century was no small matter. Disciples, through the teaching of their mentor, were to become reproductions of their master. If they failed to learn or did something publicly embarrassing, critics would look past the pupil to condemn the teacher. So, naturally, teachers took great care to choose disciples who not only had promise but who would completely submit to the teacher's instruction. A person could ask a rabbi to become his mentor, but the relationship didn't begin until the teacher extended an invitation.

After Jesus bade farewell to His guests, He began preparations for a teaching expedition through Galilee.[3] Along the shores of the sea, He would encounter His companions again and ultimately call them to become fishers of men.

See John 1:35–51.

Although the best and earliest manuscripts refer to "Bethany Beyond the Jordan" as the location of John the Baptizer's ministry (John 1:28), Origen emended the text to read "Bethabara" instead of "Bethany"—introducing an error that was accepted by Eusebius in his Onomasticon (58:18). This mistake is represented in the sixth-century Madaba Map in modern Medeba, Jordan (pictured). The top of the map is east and shows the Jordan River flowing into the Dead Sea at right. Between the Jordan River and the two houses at the bottom of the mosaic is Greek wording that reads: "Bethabara, the sanctuary of Saint John the Baptist."

Jesus named Peter "the rock." Later the Lord would reiterate this name when Peter confessed Jesus as "the Christ"—and upon Peter's rock-like confession Jesus promised to build His church. Rocks were everywhere in Israel—and still are.

Excavations at ancient Cana

THIS BEGINNING OF *His signs* JESUS DID IN CANA OF GALILEE,

AND MANIFESTED HIS GLORY, AND *His disciples believed* IN HIM.

—JOHN 2:11

OON AFTER *beginning* His public ministry, Jesus attended a wedding celebration—a lavish, weeklong feast osted by the groom's parents and attended by dozens of family and friends.

As any event planner can testify, no wedding is exempt from Murphy's Law. Groomsmen faint. Bridesmaids trip. ing bearers pick their noses. Cakes fall. And, in the case of this family in Cana of Galilee, someone failed to order nough wine—a humiliating *faux pas* in that day and culture. When Jesus's mother discovered the problem, she lerted her son without hesitation. And after brief exchange, she left the impossible situation in His care. She instructed he servants, "Whatever He says to you, do it," and then returned to the party.

Jesus could have remedied the shortage of wine by any number of means, but, perhaps with a wink and a mile, He chose to do in reality what pagan conjurors in heathen temples could only simulate. And no one could ispute the miracle. While Jesus stood back, the servants chose the vessels and filled them with water to the very op. Then, somewhere between the stone jar and the wine steward, the miraculous transformation took place. No ramatic announcement, no "voilà," no tricks, no applause. Jesus simply and quietly exercised His divine prerogative nd transformed an embarrassing situation into a social triumph for the groom's family. No one would have suffered reatly if He had not acted; the issue at stake was not of monumental importance—some might have even called it rivial. Nevertheless, the impossible predicament of His friends was important to Jesus.

Interestingly, John chose to call the event a "sign." Upon seeing Jesus use His power to accomplish a simple act of indness, His disciples' faith grew deeper.[4]

See John 2:1–11.

Mary's request for wine from Jesus may have stemmed from the prophecy that the blessing of Messiah's kingdom will be symbolized by much wine (Genesis 49:11–12). If so, Jesus's response was fitting reminder: "My hour has not yet come" (John 2:4).

"Water-pots were to supply water for the washings usual at feasts (Mark 7:4). The Jews were regarded ceremonially unclean if they did not wash both before and after eating. . . . The pots would hold about twenty gallons each, and the whole capacity would be about one hundred and twenty gallons."[5]

A Year of Popularity . . .

Passover of AD 30 to Passover of AD 31

The northern shore of the Sea of Galilee

Ruins from Chorazin

MANY OTHER *signs* JESUS ALSO PERFORMED . . .
BUT THESE HAVE BEEN WRITTEN *so that you may believe*
THAT JESUS IS THE CHRIST, THE SON OF GOD; AND THAT BELIEVING
you may have life IN HIS NAME.

— JOHN 20:30 – 31

A Year of Popularity

ANCIENT CONJURORS CREATED THE *illusion* of miracles to keep their followers coming to them with money. They mimicked the supernatural to position themselves in the minds of others as having special access to a realm that exercised dominion over the world and determined the fate of those who hoped to pass from here to there. They trafficked in the fear of the unknown.

Jesus performed miraculous signs for a very different purpose. His miracles provided relief from pain and fear; they taught of a God who cares deeply about the suffering of people and who heals for free. Jesus performed many more miracles than are described in the Gospels (John 20:30), and His motivation for these miracles was rooted in compassion.

Viewing His miracles as a whole, the astonishing power of Jesus should be a source of comfort. The matters we or the world might consider trivial, He cares about and wants to remedy. He longs to relieve our worries and has promised to supply our most fundamental needs. He has dominion over illness, tragedy, chaos, and death. And His power is not limited by time, distance, superstition, prejudice, or even the forces of evil. He taught by way of His miracles of raising the dead that evil may win a few skirmishes on earth, but only He wields everlasting power. Our fleeting seventy to eighty years in these bodies of disease and eventual death are but a twinkling compared to the magnificent and endless delights God has promised those who believe.

When you read of these authentic miracles Jesus performed, you are left with an opportunity to respond to the One who performed them. John wrote that he recorded Jesus's miracles "so that you may believe" that He is, in fact, the Son of God.[1]

See Matthew 11:20–23; John 20:30–31.

Jesus did more miracles in Chorazin (pictured here), Capernaum, and Bethsaida than in any other towns (Matthew 11:20–23). Jesus's miracles proved that the kingdom He was offering was something He could deliver. Each miracle, in addition to being the result of the Lord's kindness, also offered a preview of the permanent healing that would occur when Christ's kingdom would come on earth.

Strong tradition points to this location in Capernaum (under the building) as being where Peter's house stood. If so, Jesus healed Peter's mother-in-law here (Mark 1:30–31).

Jerusalem at night

FOR *God so loved* THE WORLD, THAT *He gave* HIS ONLY BEGOTTEN SON, THAT *whoever believes* IN HIM SHALL NOT PERISH, BUT HAVE *eternal life.*

— JOHN 3:16

JESUS SPUN NICODEMUS ON HIS HEELS WITH THE *words*, "You must be born again" (John 3:7). Birth from above, like physical birth, is not something that can be earned, deserved, or worked for. You can't pray long and hard to receive it. You can't clean up your life enough to make it possible. And you don't join a church to be born from above. All of that is just as nonsensical as a baby saying that he decided to form himself within his mother's womb.

Nicodemus was looking for the Messiah to rescue Israel from Rome and bring His people fabulous abundance. It was horizontal thinking. By saying that one must be born of water (repentance) and spirit ("from above"), Jesus tried to give Nicodemus's vision of God's kingdom a more vertical dimension. In other words, it's as if Jesus said, *"Nicodemus, this is not something you can analyze or work your way through. It involves the supernatural—the work of God inside a person."*

As the conversation turned to focus on the work of the Holy Spirit, the dialogue between Jesus and Nicodemus became very interesting. Because Nicodemus was a seasoned student of Moses, Jesus drew upon Nicodemus's knowledge of Hebrew history—specifically an event recorded in

Numbers 21:4–9. God's discipline of His rebellious people came in the form of venomous snakes, from which a number of people were killed. The Lord responded with a specific set of instructions. God told Moses to fashion a bronze snake and put it on a pole so that anyone who was bitten could look up at it. Once a person saw the snake, the venom in his or her body lost its effectiveness. Therefore, Jesus used this episode in Israel's history as an analogy: "As Moses lifted up the serpent in the wilderness, even so must the Son of Man be lifted up" (John 3:14).

Located on Mount Nebo in modern-day Jordan, this statue depicts the serpent that Moses lifted up in the wilderness—but its cross-like shape connects it to Jesus.

To what was Jesus referring? The cross, of course! The cross, where He paid the complete payment for all sin—sin past, sin present, sin future. All sin. Yours, mine, all.

Having added a new dimension to the old teacher's thinking, Jesus then gave Nicodemus a clear, direct statement of His divine mission: "For God so loved the world, that He gave His only begotten Son, that whoever believes in Him shall not perish, but have eternal life" (John 3:16).

The abundance Jesus offers is a spiritual abundance that transcends circumstances such as income, health, living conditions, and even death. The abundant life is eternal.[2]

See John 3:1–21.

Byzantine believers held that this grotto at the base of the Mount of Olives is the place where Jesus left His disciples the night He prayed in the surrounding garden of Gethsemane (Matthew 26:38). If so, Jesus stayed here often when in Jerusalem (John 18:1–2), and it may have been here that Nicodemus met Jesus at night.

The shoreline of Tabgha, beside the Sea of Galilee, where Jesus first called Peter

Do not fear, FROM NOW ON YOU WILL BE *catching men.*

— LUKE 5:10

Jesus had been *teaching* and *healing* His way through the countryside of Galilee when He began preaching to a crowd along the banks of the sea.

Peter recognized Him immediately. Jesus was the Messiah and wanted to use one of the boats as a speaking platform, which was a brilliant idea from an orator's point of view. The calm water and the indentation of the shoreline created a natural amphitheater with remarkably good acoustics. Peter ordered his crew to roll up the nets, load them back onto the boat, and row a short distance from the shore.

Jesus concluded His lesson and dismissed the people, at which point Peter expected He would want to be let off on land. But the rabbi looked at Peter and said, "Put out into the deep water and let down your nets for a catch." Simon replied, "Master, we worked hard all night and caught nothing, but I will do as You say and let down the nets" (Luke 5:4–5).

The haul of fish nearly sank Peter's boat and that of James and John, who came alongside to help. The object lesson brought Peter to his knees. Of the rock-solid fisherman, Luke wrote, "Amazement had seized him" (5:9), and Peter's next act reveals a dawning awareness that Jesus was no ordinary man: "He fell down at Jesus' feet, saying, 'Go away from me Lord, for I am a sinful man!'" (5:8).

The Sea of Galilee is home to a variety of species of fish: sardines, musht, and barbels, or tilapia, also known today as "St. Peter's Fish."

Sinfulness cannot survive in the presence of divine glory. Because Peter understood himself to be a man tainted with sin, he feared Jesus. As Peter, John, and John's brother James trembled before their Messiah, they heard the words that would forever change their lives: "Do not fear, from now on you will be catching men" (5:10).

That very moment, Peter leaped after the Messiah's call: "Follow Me, and I will make you become fishers of men" (Mark 1:17). Peter didn't know where the call led, what adventures it promised, or what dangers it entailed. People asked, but he didn't know. And he didn't care how foolish his neighbors thought him to be. He cast himself on the call of Jesus with wanton gusto, determined to ride it to the end.[3]

See Luke 5:1–11.

Fishing has always been a major industry on the Sea of Galilee. The area where the miraculous catch occurred is called in Greek, Hepta-pegon, meaning "place of seven springs." Its Arabic name is Tabgha (pronounced, "tav-guh"). The springs stir up algae in this part of the sea, drawing fish from the entire lake. Fishermen still frequent the location today.

WHEN *Jesus*
saw him LYING THERE,

AND KNEW THAT

HE HAD ALREADY BEEN

A LONG TIME IN THAT

CONDITION, HE SAID TO

HIM, *"Do you wish*

TO GET WELL?"

—JOHN 5:6

A Year of Popularity

The Pool of Bethesda in Jerusalem

WE TEND TO *think* that the longer something is true, the more difficult it is to change—perhaps because time has a way of cementing reality in our minds and forming an impenetrable barrier against hope. Traditions and superstitions become cemented over several generations and can have the same mind-numbing effect.

When Jesus arrived in Jerusalem to celebrate one of the Jewish feasts, He visited the Pool of Bethesda (John 5:2–3). This complex of two pools surrounded by five colonnades lay just below the northeast corner of Herod's temple and appears to have been a religious sanitarium, called an *asclepieion*. The Greeks believed Asclepius, the god of medicine and healing, to be a kind, gentle savior to the infirm.

During His visit, Jesus came upon a man who had been debilitated by disease for nearly four decades—a lifetime in those days. Apparently, superstition promised that the stirring of the waters brought special healing to those who could make their way in. But the man was alone, and in a cruel twist of irony, the race for a spot in the pool went to the able-bodied

first. Of all the hopeless cases in the sanitarium, none rivaled his. How many nights did the man plead for a visit from Asclepius? How many days did he lay there in the shadow of the temple, helplessly watching for the stirring of the waters?

Again without fanfare, without crowd-pleasing predictions, Jesus simply instructed the man, "Stand up! Pick up your mat and walk" (5:8 NET). Immediately, atrophied bones and muscles grew strong and lifted the man to his feet for the first time in decades. Time may have cemented this man's fate in the mind of the community. They certainly had relegated him to the sanitarium, so his striding into the temple later that day must have come as a shock to everyone.

By this time, the temple leaders were beginning to take notice. This was no mere upstart rabbi from the backwaters of Galilee.[4]

See John 5.

The Pool of Bethesda today lies alongside the Crusader's Church of St. Anne, at the northeast corner of the Temple Mount in Jerusalem. Archaeologists have uncovered two pools that were surrounded in total by a colonnade that also ran down the middle, providing "five porticoes" (John 5:2). Bethesda means "house of mercy."

The Greek god Asclepius was the god of healing. Medical facilities (called asclepieion*) would often adjoin places of worship, though it is doubtful Asclepius was worshiped in Jerusalem so near the Jewish temple. Even today, Asclepius's Staff remains a symbol of medicine.*

A Year of Transition . . .

Passover of AD 31 to Passover of AD 32

The Sea of Galilee

"Look, why are they doing what is not lawful on the Sabbath?" (Mark 2:24). The Pharisees' question in relation to Jesus's disciples' actions stemmed from the rabbinic tradition that picking, rubbing, and eating grain amounted to working to prepare a meal. Thus, the disciples were pigeonholed as breaking the Sabbath.

The Pharisees WERE SAYING TO HIM, "LOOK, WHY ARE THEY

DOING WHAT IS *not lawful* ON THE SABBATH?"

—MARK 2:24

IN FIRST-CENTURY *Israel*, two primary groups vied for religious control over Israel, which kept them locked in a symbiotic love-hate relationship with each other: the aristocratic Sadducees and the nationalistic Pharisees. Of the two things needed to manipulate a people—a religious institution and a religious authority—neither party had both. So they jealously guarded what they controlled.

To maintain moral superiority—or at least the impression of it—the Pharisees chose to emphasize the portion of God's Law that suited their natural inclinations. For whatever reason, the fourth commandment in relation to observing the Sabbath became their favorite (Exodus 20:10–11).

Originally, the seventh day was set aside to commemorate God's creation of the world and to celebrate His provision. In six days, He fashioned the earth and filled it with everything humankind would need. On the seventh, He stopped all activity. *Sabbath* is based on the Hebrew verb that means "to cease."

The Sabbath was a day for feasting and singing, a time in which families delighted in their God and bonded with one another. But something curious happened when the armies of Babylon destroyed the temple in 586 BC and carried the Jews away from their land. Having been stripped of all that made them distinctly Hebrew, they looked to the Law of Moses to restore their national identity and to bind them together as a people. Thus, the exile gave birth to Pharisaism, which made legalism the core value of Judaism and Jewish identity.

By the time of Jesus, the Pharisees had transformed the Sabbath into something very different from what God had ordained. To the simple command, "rest," the Pharisees added a long list of specific prohibitions. And, just in case they had overlooked something, they established thirty-nine categories of forbidden activity: carrying, burning, extinguishing, finishing, writing, erasing, cooking, washing, sewing, tearing, knotting, untying, shaping, plowing, planting, reaping, harvesting, threshing, winnowing, selecting, sifting, grinding, kneading, combing, spinning, dyeing, chain stitching, warping, weaving, unraveling, building, demolishing, trapping, shearing, slaughtering, skinning, tanning, smoothing, and marking.[1]

How strange that resting should be so burdensome! No one dared to challenge the Pharisees' exclusive jurisdiction as police, judge, and jury over all matters related to the Sabbath. No one, that is, until Jesus.

See Mark 2:23–28.

Alfred Edersheim relates that "according to the Talmud . . . there were at least two . . . acts involved: that of plucking the ears of corn, ranged under the sin of reaping, and that of rubbing them, which might be ranged under sifting in a sieve, threshing, sifting out fruit, grinding, or fanning."[2]

The "Sower's Cove" beside the Sea of Galilee

"I SPEAK TO THEM *in parables*; BECAUSE WHILE SEEING THEY *do not see*, AND WHILE HEARING THEY *do not hear*, NOR DO THEY UNDERSTAND."

— MATTHEW 13:13

JESUS BEGAN *to teach* the people in parables. When the Twelve asked Jesus why, He replied, "I speak to them in parables; because while seeing they do not see, and while hearing they do not hear, nor do they understand" (Matthew 13:13). Matthew later added: "He did not speak to [the crowds] without a parable" (13:34). The parables of Jesus allowed the observers to see what their hearts chose to see, which was determined by how they responded to Jesus. The first parable Jesus told illustrates this truth.

The Lord sat down in a little boat by the seashore and talked about a farmer who dropped seeds into the dirt (Matthew 13:1–9). Simple story. Easy to remember, even if you're a little kid. Same seed, different soil. Same time of sowing, but different results, to be exact.

Unlike most parables He told, Jesus went back over this one point by point. He left no room for doubt or misunderstanding. First, the seed represents "the word of the kingdom" (13:19). Second, the different soils—the road, the rocks, the thorns, and the good soil—represent people's varied responses to that "word." Next, the results are directly related to the condition of the soil . . . not the quality of the seed. Same seed, remember, but different soil.

Being the great communicator that He was, the Nazarene left much of the application unsaid. He was careful not to smother His listeners, rather to bait them, to have each person draw his or her own specific conclusions.

Interestingly, Jesus closed His brief talk with the familiar line, "He who has ears, let him hear" (13:9), almost as if He assumed, "You're gonna miss what I'm saying if you don't let these things penetrate . . . hear them well . . . absorb their significance . . . don't let anything drown out My voice!"

Jesus is still communicating, but if we're not careful, we'll let our many distractions prevent us from having ears to hear.[3]

See Matthew 13:1–23.

Tradition holds that Jesus taught His famous "Parable of the Soils" to a crowd on this hillside while He Himself sat in a boat just offshore (Matthew 13:1–2). An acoustical study published in Biblical Archaeologist *revealed that between five and seven thousand people could gather below the road and clearly hear a lone speaker.[4] Twice that number could fit on the whole hillside and still hear a voice on the shore.*

The Plain of Bethsaida, the location of the feeding of the five thousand

"WHERE ARE WE TO BUY BREAD, SO THAT THESE MAY EAT?"
THIS [JESUS] WAS SAYING *to test him*, FOR HE HIMSELF KNEW

WHAT HE WAS INTENDING TO DO.

—JOHN 6:5–6

J ESUS HAD BEEN *teaching* throughout the region of Galilee when He decided to take His disciples away from the crowds to enjoy the solitude of the hill country northeast of the Sea of Galilee.

But His fame had grown far and fast. As He taught His inner circle of pupils, a multitude began to gather. People—thousands of them—followed their Messiah and gave no thought to provision. They quite possibly expected that He would provide for them.

Eventually, five thousand men and their families had gathered. Jesus tugged on Philip's sleeve and asked, "Where are we to buy bread, so that these may eat?" (John 6:5). The question, of course, was the beginning of a lesson. Jesus had chosen the Twelve and had been training them to assume leadership in the new kingdom. Like a true mentor, He was gently pushing His men to the forefront and allowing them to meet the challenges of ministry. Regrettably, learning often comes on the heels of failure.

Philip tallied the people and estimated the cost of bread. His mental calculator kicked in: "Two hundred denarii worth of bread is not sufficient for them" (6:7). Meanwhile, Andrew told Jesus, "There is a lad here who has five barley loaves and two fish, but what are these for so many people?" (6:9).

Perhaps with a twinkle in His eye and a reassuring nod, Jesus said, "Have the people sit down" (6:10). The disciples divided the multitude into groups and arranged an efficient distribution plan as Jesus gave thanks for the provision and began breaking the bread and pulling off pieces of fish . . . again and again and yet again. For hours, He multiplied the humble offering of the little boy and passed the abundance to a brigade of disciples.

At the end of the day, the lesson should have been clear. The size of a challenge should never be measured in terms of what we have to offer. It will never be enough. Furthermore, provision is God's responsibility, not ours. We are merely called to commit what we have—even if it's no more than a sack lunch.[5]

See John 6:1–13.

Byzantine believers in the mid-fifth century commemorated the miracle with a beautiful mosaic, now preserved within the modern-day Church of the Multiplication of the Loaves and Fishes. Except for the resurrection, the feeding of the five thousand is the only miracle that appears in all four gospels. Why so significant? Jesus was beginning to show His disciples how to do ministry in the anticipated era of the church.

Church of the Multiplication of the Loaves and Fishes

Rough waters on the Sea of Galilee

AT ABOUT THE FOURTH WATCH OF THE NIGHT

HE CAME TO THEM, *walking* ON THE SEA.

—MARK 6:48

An ancient mosaic, depicting a first-century boat

This ancient boat was discovered in the Sea of Galilee in 1986 and dates from the time of Christ. In fact, the fishing boat could hold up to fifteen men — the type of boat Jesus's fishermen-disciples would have owned. Winds descending the hills that surround the shallow Sea of Galilee can still stir up storms with no warning.

AFTER JESUS *fed* THE MULTITUDE, the crowd rose up and began discussing how they could remove the present government and make Jesus their king (John 6:15). Because Jesus disapproved of their plan and rejected their motives, He commanded the people to disperse. He quickly withdrew further into the hills. Meanwhile, His disciples prepared the boat as He had commanded and set sail for Capernaum ahead of Him.

As Jesus enjoyed a few hours of solitude, the frenzy of the crowd died down, allowing Him time to relax and reflect. But by then, a fierce squall had descended on the sea.

The men had been rowing against the wind and straining at the oars for more than three miles when Jesus decided to rescue them. He walked down the mountain to the shore and straight across the top of the water. As He approached the ship, the men quite naturally didn't know what to make of the figure coming toward them.

> But when they saw Him walking on the sea, they supposed that it was a ghost, and cried out; for they all saw Him and were terrified. But immediately He spoke with them and said to them, "Take courage; it is I, do not be afraid." Then He got into the boat with them, and the wind stopped; and they were utterly astonished, for they had not gained any insight from the incident of the loaves, but their heart was hardened. (Mark 6:49–52)

In the disciples' day and culture, a person described as having a "hard heart" didn't mean he or she was unkind or cruel but that this person's reasoning and emotions had become resistant to development. We might say, "hard-headed." Even after witnessing Jesus perform the astonishing miracle on the hillside earlier that day, the disciples failed to put all the clues together.

Jesus walked on the very sea that threatened to pull the disciples under. He commanded the wind that tossed their boat around like a toy. He spoke a word, and the storm instantly ceased its fury. Who but God can control the weather?[6]

See Mark 6:45–52.

The Capernaum Synagogue

THESE THINGS HE SAID IN THE *synagogue*

AS HE TAUGHT IN CAPERNAUM.

—JOHN 6:59

B ECAUSE MANY OF THE PEOPLE WERE *following* J ESUS only to find their next meal, Jesus used a fate-sealing word picture to thin out the crowd: "Truly, truly, I say to you, unless you eat the flesh of the Son of Man and drink His blood, you have no life in yourselves" (John 6:53). This, of course, was Jesus stating metaphorically that He would sacrifice Himself to provide eternal life for anyone who would receive it.

Nothing would be the same after that. If Jesus had been running for political office, His campaign manager would have resigned. That day in Capernaum, Jesus divided His core constituency and alienated the majority. The political experts among the Twelve put their heads in their hands as they saw their future in Israel's new government go up in smoke.

But Jesus didn't come to win the approval of people or to swing the majority of a disenfranchised voter base to embrace His platform and sweep Him into a position of power in Jerusalem. He came to speak "the solemn truth." And let's face it; the truth is rarely popular. In fact, it usually offends the majority.

Speaking of that, it was at this time many left Jesus. He was not the Messiah they were looking for. Jesus turned to the Twelve and asked, "You do not want to go away also, do you?" (6:67). Peter said, in effect, "Lord, we don't exactly understand everything You just said, but You're our only hope. We have nowhere else to turn. We've chosen You, and that's that."

These were the sweetest, most authentic words a disciple could have spoken.

Jesus responded by clarifying a subtle point and revealing a chilling insight, "Did I Myself not choose you, the twelve, and yet one of you is a devil?" (6:70). The cosmic battle between good and evil divides heart from heart and, on that day, a subtle crack—barely a sliver—formed within one of their number.[7]

See John 6:24–71.

The white marble synagogue in Capernaum dates after Christ's time, but it sits on the basalt foundation of the synagogue of Jesus's day. It was here Christ performed an exorcism and taught the words of life found in Mark 1:21–27 and John 6:35–59.

The Final Year: Looking Ahead to Jerusalem . . .

Passover of AD 32 to Passover of AD 33

Jerusalem

Jesus's conflict with the religious leaders over tradition took place in Galilee.

"WHY DO YOUR DISCIPLES *break the tradition* OF THE ELDERS? FOR THEY DO NOT *wash their hands* WHEN THEY EAT BREAD."

—MATTHEW 15:2

WHILE JESUS WAS STILL *ministering* IN GALILEE, an envoy of Pharisees traveled from Jerusalem to meet with Him on a matter of grave concern to them. "Why do Your disciples break the tradition of the elders? For they do not wash their hands when they eat bread" (Matthew 15:2).

This wasn't an issue of hygiene but of the tedious rules of tradition. The religious leaders followed a practice that required them to meticulously wash their hands before eating, lest they themselves become ritually defiled. The "tradition of the elders" represented the customs and detailed rules of behavior derived from rabbinic interpretation of Old Testament Law (Mark 7:8–9, 13; Galatians 1:14; Colossians 2:8). In the time of Christ, these traditions were mostly oral, but they would become codified more than one hundred years later and form what is called the *Mishnah*. In this "tradition of the elders," a single command in the Old Testament may have hundreds of specific applications, such as the way one washed his or her hands before eating a meal.

The Pharisees viewed this oral tradition as having authority *on par with Scripture*. Jesus's answer is classic:

> And He answered and said to them, "Why do you yourselves transgress the commandment of God for the sake of your tradition? . . . You hypocrites, rightly did Isaiah prophesy of you: 'This people honors Me with their lips, but their heart is far away from Me. But in vain do they worship Me, teaching as doctrines the precepts of men.'" (Matthew 15:3, 7–9)

Tradition is not divinely inspired. The precepts of men are not the doctrines of God. They never will be! After Jesus offered this stinging rebuke, the disciples asked the obvious: "Do You know that the Pharisees were offended when they heard this statement?" (Matthew 15:12).

You think?

The Pharisees always took offense to truth. These types of people still do today. When a sense of personal preference lords over biblical priorities, the worship of God is vain and meaningless. Why? Because it's really the worship of self.[1]

See Matthew 15.

Alfred Edersheim captured the tedium of the Pharisees' rite: "The water was poured on both hands, which must be free of anything covering them, such as gravel, mortar, etc. The hands were lifted up, so as to make the water run to the wrist, in order to ensure that the whole hand was washed, and that the water polluted by the hand did not again run down the fingers. Similarly, each hand was rubbed with the other (the fist), provided the hand that rubbed had been affused: otherwise, the rubbing might be done against the head, or even against a wall."[2]

Banias Falls, near Caesarea Philippi

He said to them, "But *who* do you say that I am?"
Simon Peter answered, "You are *the Christ,*
the Son of the living God."

— MATTHEW 16:15 –16

AT THE *zenith* OF HIS CAREER, Jesus pulled away toward the secluded area of Caesarea Philippi. On His mind was a crucial question for His disciples.

The surroundings were impressive. Flowing springs. Lush gardens. Monuments and temples dedicated to the worship of the Greek god Pan lined the pathways. A massive, white marble temple to Caesar loomed tall. Jesus leaned forward and said perhaps rather quietly to a small handful of men, "Who do the people say that the Son of Man is?" (Matthew 16:13).

Jesus was posing an opinion-poll question about Himself. "What's the buzz?" He asked. According to verse 14, the disciples responded spontaneously, "Some say John the Baptist." By now, John was dead, having been beheaded by Herod Antipas. Some people were saying that Jesus was John the Baptist raised from the dead. That's why He had miraculous powers.

The disciples continued, "Some say . . . Elijah." Elijah had died hundreds of years earlier. For centuries, the Jews viewed Elijah as the prince of the prophets, the one who would be the forerunner, but not the Messiah. And a third answer came: "Some say . . . Jeremiah, or one of the prophets" (16:14). These on-the-street opinions all boiled down to this answer: "He's a man."

Then Jesus narrowed His gaze and personalized the question for His men: "But who do *you* say that I am?" (16:15, emphasis added). Even though the question was addressed to the group, Peter spoke for all of them. That's like Peter, isn't it? His answer is wonderful: "You are the Christ, the Son of the living God" (16:16).

We have at times laughed at Simon Peter. But here's a moment when we must salute him. Christ is the flesh-and-bone God, not a fixed-in-stone god. And notice the definite articles. His response wasn't a generalized series of wild guesses. This wasn't public opinion talking. This is a specific answer about *the* Messiah, *the* Son of *the* living God.

Can you picture the scene? Peter didn't always get it right, but he nailed it this time![3]

See Matthew 16:13–19.

The spring that flowed from this cave still supplies part of the headwaters of the Jordan River. Pagan worship, including the worship of the god Pan, occurred here by throwing sacrifices into the cave. The Arabic language cannot enunciate Ps, so the ancient name for the site, Panias, has been corrupted into the Arabic transliteration, Banias, the name of the site today.

Niches held statues of the Greek god Pan.

Caesarea Philippi

He turned and *said to Peter*, "Get behind Me, *Satan!*

You are a stumbling block to Me; for you are not setting

your mind on *God's interests*, but man's."

— Matthew 16:23

JESUS'S WORDS WERE *aimed at the devil . . .* but the Lord spoke them directly to Peter: "Get behind Me, Satan! You are a stumbling block to Me; for you are not setting your mind on God's interests, but man's" (Matthew 16:23). Jesus had just promised that He would build His church on Simon Peter's foundational, rock-like confession that Jesus is the Christ.

Right after these momentous words, Jesus told His disciples something they had never heard before. He predicted His own imminent death and resurrection. But Peter would have none of it. *How could the Messiah die? Unthinkable!* So Peter took Jesus aside and began to rebuke Him (16:13–22).

Can you imagine rebuking Jesus?

Cave of Pan

Satan had tempted Peter to set his mind on humanity's interests rather than on God's. No sooner had Jesus promised to build His church than the Adversary went to work trying to crumble its foundation. Remarkable! Jesus immediately confronted the threat with those strong words to Satan, and Peter never forgot them.

About a year later, Peter would have a similar incident to remember. When Jesus and His disciples ate the Last Supper in the Upper Room, Peter announced that he would go with Jesus to prison and to death. But Jesus turned to Peter and said that three times Peter would deny even knowing Jesus. Again, Peter would refuse association with a suffering Savior. He would set his mind on humanity's interests rather than on God's. Jesus's words to Peter reveal the source of this temptation (and should send a chill up our backs): "Simon, Simon, behold, Satan has demanded permission to sift you like wheat" (Luke 22:31).

It's no surprise, then, that it was Peter who would later write to warn his fellow Christians of the hard lesson he himself had learned more than once: "Be of sober spirit, be on the alert. Your adversary, the devil, prowls around like a roaring lion, seeking someone to devour" (1 Peter 5:8).[4]

Jesus mentioned His death for the first time, and Peter's response represented the feelings of all the disciples. He outright rejected it. Jesus's ensuing words to Peter—and Peter's words to us—reveal that the primary enemy of our souls is Satan—who works to focus our attention on human interests rather than on God's. Sometimes God puts crosses in our paths.

See Matthew 16:20–27.

In the region of Caesarea Philippi, Jesus uttered a word He had never used before: church. How ironic that this revelation to His disciples would not occur in Israel but in a pagan, Gentile land. Peter would later share the good news of Christ to the first Gentile convert, Cornelius, in a town with a similar name—Caesarea by the Sea (Acts 10).

Mount Hermon

AND *He was transfigured* BEFORE THEM; AND *His face* SHONE LIKE THE SUN, AND *His garments* BECAME AS WHITE AS LIGHT.

— MATTHEW 17:2

SIX DAYS AFTER THE SCENE NEAR *Caesarea Philippi*—after revealing His imminent death in Jerusalem—Jesus gave to Peter, James, and John affirmation of His glory, divine nature, and coming kingdom (Matthew 16:28–17:8). The text says Jesus was "transfigured" on the mountain (17:2; Mark 9:2). Jesus revealed His true glory, which His flesh had concealed just as the veil of the tabernacle had hidden God's glory (Hebrews 10:20).

Suddenly, Moses and Elijah also made glorious cameo appearances. They spoke of Jesus's "departure" at Jerusalem, the very event Jesus had just revealed to His disciples in Caesarea Philippi (Luke 9:31). Peter blurted: "Lord, it is good for us to be here; if You wish, I will make three tabernacles here, one for You, and one for Moses, and one for Elijah" (Matthew 17:4). What was Peter suggesting? The prophet Zechariah had written that when the Messiah reigns on the earth, He will require all nations to come and celebrate Sukkot—the Feast of Booths, or Feast of the Tabernacles (Zechariah 14:16–19). Peter was pushing for the kingdom to begin!

But even before Peter could finish his words, God the Father interrupted: "This is My beloved Son, with whom I am well-pleased; listen to Him!" (Matthew 17:5).

The disciples fell face-down in a coil of terror.

The transfiguration confirmed that Jesus was the Messiah who would come in glory, but the way to glory would come through the cross. There was no going around it. Even in the presence of Christ's glory on the mountain, Moses and Elijah spoke of Christ's death, or "departure"—literally, in the Greek, His *exodus* (Luke 9:31)—a nice literary touch with Moses standing there.

Surely Jesus's disciples recalled His recent words, "If anyone wishes

A modern-day "tabernacle" used to celebrate Sukkot

to come after Me, he must deny himself, and take up his cross and follow Me" (Matthew 16:24). Although we don't carry literal wooden crosses, Jesus's metaphor still demands a literal application of the struggle God calls us each to bear. Our crosses represent the difficult obedience God requires daily.

Notice also the order of events: as a man, Jesus went to the cross *before* He experienced the joys of glory. When will we learn that it can be no different for us?[5]

See Matthew 16:24–17:8.

Jesus brought three of His disciples up on the slopes of a "high mountain," probably Mount Hermon, which towered above the pagan area of Caesarea Philippi.

The Pool of Siloam was discovered by accident in 2004. Archaeologists uncovered only a portion of this lower pool, exposing the entire north side — more than 225 feet long.

"THE MAN WHO IS CALLED *Jesus*
made clay, AND ANOINTED MY EYES, AND SAID TO ME,
'*Go to Siloam* AND WASH';
SO I WENT AWAY AND WASHED, AND *I received sight.*"

—JOHN 9:11

Imagine THE SCENE. The man was well known in his community because of his blindness. His begging for alms had made him a notable figure around the temple for years, perhaps decades. Pharisees judged him and Sadducees ignored him; some worshipers showed compassion while others clutched their purses and tiptoed by.

Then, one day, this same man strode into the temple without his stick and beggar's basket, his eyes feasting on the splendor of God's house and savoring every detail. Worshipers in the temple courtyard noticed the familiar face but struggled to make sense of what they saw.

> "Is not this the one who used to sit and beg?" Others were saying, "This is he," still others were saying, "No, but he is like him." He kept saying, "I am the one." So they were saying to him, "How then were your eyes opened?" He answered, "The man who is called Jesus made clay, and anointed my eyes, and said to me, 'Go to Siloam and wash'; so I went away and washed, and I received sight." They said to him, "Where is He?" He said, "I do not know." (John 9:8–12)

At this point in the story, we would expect someone to make plans for a huge celebration. But the Pharisees, upon discovering the man had been healed on the Sabbath, nitpicked, grumbled, and debated. The Pharisees had, as usual, failed to see the big picture. Their blindness would be comical were it not so tragic and their example so influential.

Jesus had declared, "I am the Light of the world," and then He had given the man sight (John 9:5–7). In this one act, Jesus demonstrated power over disabilities, sin, bad theology, the temple, the Sabbath, and the skeptics—especially the self-absorbed Pharisees who opposed Him. He had this opportunity because a baby came into the world without the ability to see.

The man was not blind because he or his parents sinned. He was blind because he was born into a world that has been twisted by sin. Furthermore, God gave the baby's congenital disability a divine purpose before the world ever began.[6]

See John 9.

For many years, the Pool of Siloam was thought to be the upper pool beside the exit of Hezekiah's Tunnel (pictured). Discovered near the turn of the twentieth century, this pool dates only to the fifth century AD.

The Siloam Inscription, written in the Hebrew script of Hezekiah's day

Modern-day Bethany

JESUS SAID TO HER, *"I am the resurrection*

AND THE LIFE; HE WHO BELIEVES IN ME

will live EVEN IF HE DIES."

— JOHN 11:25

A VERY CLOSE *friend* OF JESUS'S NAMED LAZARUS contracted a fatal illness and lay dying in his home at Bethany, a town near Jerusalem in Judea. The man's sisters, Martha and Mary, sent a messenger to Jesus to let Him know that His friend was very sick, but Jesus waited for days before starting out. By the time He reached Bethany, Lazarus had been in the grave four days.

Martha bitterly complained, "Lord, if You had been here, my brother would not have died. Even now I know that whatever You ask of God, God will give You" (John 11:21–22). Shortly thereafter, Jesus stood before the burial cave that held the body of His friend. Without hesitation, He commanded, "Remove the stone" (11:39).

first-century tomb in Israel that is similar to a tomb in which Lazarus would have been buried (note the rolling stone).

Then Jesus raised His eyes, and said, "Father, I thank You that You have heard Me. I knew that You always hear Me; but because of the people standing around I said it, so that they may believe that You sent Me." When He had said these things, He cried out with a loud voice, "Lazarus, come forth." The man who had died came forth. (11:41–44)

What a remarkable reunion that must have been! As Jesus stood back and watched the family embracing, weeping with joy, surely He smiled. His silence is eloquent.

In the words of an old gospel song, it was "a foretaste of glory divine." As Lazarus's family and friends celebrated his return from the dead, they enjoyed a brief taste of a future feast Jesus promised to bring the world. Sin may have the power to kill and destroy, but God is the creator of life. He can create it from nothing, and He can restore it from death. The reassurance Jesus gave Martha is the same promise He extends to the world: "I am the resurrection and the life; he who believes in Me will live even if he dies, and everyone who lives and believes in Me will never die" (11:25–26).[7]

See John 11.

Nineteenth-century stained glass window in the Nikolai Church in Örebro by Carl Almquist

Storm clouds over modern-day Jerusalem

"What are we doing? For *this man* is performing many signs. If we let Him go on like this, *all men will believe in Him,* and the Romans will come and take away both our place and our nation."

— JOHN 11:47 – 48

FOR MANY MONTHS, *storm clouds* HAD BEEN GATHERING over Jerusalem. Jesus focused His attention on Galilee during the early part of His ministry, but He regularly traveled to the Holy City in Judea to celebrate the more than half-dozen Jewish feasts throughout the year. And each visit intensified the growing tension between Jesus and the religious establishment— both the Sadducees, who held control of the temple, and the Pharisees, who had a grip on the people.

The disciples could sense the danger mounting. So when Jesus announced that they would travel to visit Martha and Mary in the village of Bethany, just two miles from Jerusalem, Thomas turned to the other disciples and shrugged, "Let us also go, so that we may die with Him" (John 11:16). The disciples' fear was not unfounded. On their last visit, an angry mob sought to stone their Master.

After Jesus raised Lazarus from the dead, He won a new assembly of followers. However, several friends of the Pharisees saw His growing popularity as a threat and scurried to Jerusalem with the news.

> Therefore the chief priests and the Pharisees convened a council, and were saying, "What are we doing? For this man is performing many signs. If we let Him go on like this, all men will believe in Him, and the Romans will come and take away both our place and our nation." But one of them, Caiaphas, who was high priest that year, said to them, "You know nothing at all, nor do you take into account that it is expedient for you that one man die for the people, and that the whole nation not perish." Now he did not say this on his own initiative, but being high priest that year, he prophesied that Jesus was going to die for the nation, and not for the nation only, but in order that He might also gather together into one the children of God who are scattered abroad. (11:47–52)

With that, the plot to kill Jesus began.

The religious leaders would have to be crafty. They didn't dare seize Jesus in public for fear that the ever-growing multitude of His followers would turn on them and revolt. And nothing would bring down the wrath of Rome quicker than insurrection.[8]

See John 11:47–57.

A first-century ossuary, a stone box which permanently held the bones of the deceased after the body had decomposed for a year in a family tomb

In the first century BC, Marcus Licinius Crassus defeated the runaway slave Spartacus and his six thousand rebels and then crucified them at regular intervals along the highway leading to Spartacus's hometown. The general never issued the order to have the bodies or the crosses removed, so for years—perhaps decades—the macabre wooden memorials warned would-be revolutionaries, "This could be you."

A portion of the "Ascent of Adummim," the road Jesus walked from Jericho up to Jerusalem

"BEHOLD, WE ARE GOING *up to Jerusalem*, AND THE SON OF MAN WILL BE DELIVERED TO THE CHIEF PRIESTS AND THE SCRIBES; AND THEY WILL *condemn Him to death* AND WILL HAND HIM OVER TO THE GENTILES . . . AND THREE DAYS LATER *He will rise again*."

— MARK 10:33–34

The Final Year: Looking Ahead to Jerusalem

YOU PROBABLY KNOW WHERE THIS NARRATIVE *leads*. Before the story is over, Jesus will be crucified and, at least for a time, His disciples will be completely disillusioned, wondering, *Where did it all go wrong?*

They may have traced the unraveling of their messianic hopes to a particular day in Capernaum, when Jesus began to winnow the multitudes of His followers. Jesus, on the other hand, never regarded His path to the cross as anything but the successful unfolding of God's plan. Only a week before His crucifixion, Jesus made it plain:

> They were on the road going up to Jerusalem, and Jesus was walking on ahead of them; and they were amazed, and those who followed were fearful. And again He took the twelve aside and began to tell them what was going to happen to Him, saying, "Behold, we are going up to Jerusalem, and the Son of Man will be delivered to the chief priests and the scribes; and they will condemn Him to death and will hand Him over to the Gentiles. They will mock Him and spit on Him, and scourge Him and kill Him, and three days later He will rise again." (Mark 10:32–34)

The modern "Good Samaritan Inn," near the ancient Ascent of Adummim, remembers Jesus's parable recorded in Luke 10:30–35.

Remember the question that Jesus asked His glory-hungry disciples at Caesarea Philippi? "Who is Jesus Christ to you?" There can be no greater question you could answer as well. Your reply must be, "The Son of the living God, my Savior, and my God."

Who else could He be? There is no one else qualified to grant forgiveness but Jesus. There is no one other than Christ who will stay closer to you when everyone and everything is stripped from you. There is no one else who can turn your bitterness into relief or turn your grief into joy.

When you've taken your last breath and you step into eternity, having answered Jesus's question with faith, there is not a soul who has ever lived who will be by your side but Jesus. He alone is qualified to escort you from the grave to glory.

He alone is God.[9]

See Mark 10:32–34.

The road from Jericho up to Jerusalem bore the name, "Ascent of Adummim," meaning "ascent of the red places." Some suggest the name derived from the red rocks along the way. Eusebius of Caesarea, in the third century, connected the road with a village Tal'at ed-Damm, meaning "ascent of blood," likely because the many thieves along the way spilled the blood of travelers.

Appendix

OUTLINE OF CHRIST'S MINISTRY

An Excerpt from *Chronological Aspects of the Life of Christ*
by Harold W. Hoehner

❧

[Editor's note: While there are various views on the length of Jesus's ministry, Dr. Hoehner has provided a good summary that outlines a three-year ministry.]

The validity of the theory of Jesus's three-year ministry has good bases from both the Synoptics and the gospel of John. Therefore, the three-year ministry of Jesus from the first Passover to the passion Passover is a most viable option. Of course, since Jesus's baptism and public ministry preceded the first Passover, the total length of His ministry would be about three and a half years.

MINISTRY BEFORE THE FIRST PASSOVER

Jesus's public ministry began in the summer or autumn of AD 29. After John baptized Jesus, there was the temptation (Matthew 4:1–11; Mark 1:12–13; Luke 4:1–13); the call of His first disciples (John 1:35–51); the wedding feast at Cana of Galilee (2:1–11); His journey to Capernaum (2:12); and then His journey to Jerusalem to attend the first Passover of His ministry (2:13, 23) on Nisan 14, or April 7, AD 30.[1]

MINISTRY FROM PASSOVER OF 30 TO PASSOVER OF 31

After the Passover of AD 30, Jesus's ministry was primarily in Jerusalem (John 3:1–21) and Judea (3:22–36). With the imprisonment of John the Baptist, Jesus then moved from Judea to go to Galilee (Matthew 4:12; Mark 1:14; Luke 4:14; John 4:3). He passed through Samaria and ministered there (John 4:4–42) around January/February of AD 31 (4:35). He then moved into Galilee and ministered there (Matthew 4:13–17; Mark 1:14–15; Luke 4:14–15; John 4:43–46).

MINISTRY FROM PASSOVER OF 31 TO PASSOVER OF 32

The plucking of grain on the Sabbath (Mark 2:23–28; Luke 6:1–5 Matthew 12:1–8) would have been around the time of the second Passover of Jesus's ministry. There is the continuation of the Galilean ministry including the Sermon on the Mount and the extensive healing ministry. It may well be around the summer of 31 that Jesus was rejected by the religious leaders who attributed His ministry to Beelzebub (Matthew 12:22–37; Mark 3:19–30 after which He spoke in parables. If one accepts the feast of John 5:1 as being the Feast of Tabernacles, Jesus would have been in Jerusalem for the feast during October 21–28, AD 31.[2] Returning to Galilee, Jesus sent out the Twelve (Mark 6:6–13; Luke 9:1–6), received the news of the beheading of John the Baptist, the Twelve returned, after which He withdrew with the Twelve. This is followed by the feeding of the 5,000 (Matthew 14:13–21; Mark 6:32–44 Luke 9:10–17; John 6:1–15) around the Passover (John 6:4) of AD 32, which would have been April 13/14.[3]

MINISTRY FROM PASSOVER OF 32 TO PASSOVER OF 33

From the Passover to the Feast of Tabernacles of 32 was a period of Jesus's retirement from public ministry.[4] Shortly after the feeding of the 5,000 Jesus and His disciples withdrew to Phoenicia (Matthew 15:21–28; Mark 7:24–30 They returned via the Decapolis. This was followed by the feeding of the 4,000 (Matthew 15:32–39; Mark 8:1–10), the great confession at Caesarea-Philippi (Matthew 16:13–20; Mark 8:27–30; Luke 9:18–21), and the transfiguration (Matthew 17:1–9; Mark 9:2–10; Luke 9:28–36) as well as ministries of teaching and healing.

John states that Jesus went up to Jerusalem to the Feast of Tabernacles (John 7:2, 10) which would have been September 10–17, AD 32.[5] All three Synoptic Gospels state that Jesus went up to Jerusalem (Matthew 19:1; Mark 10:1 Luke 9:51). The real question is whether or not one can fit Luke's central section (Luke 9:51–19:28) with the gospel of John. Wieseler has suggested that the three journeys mentioned in John (John 7:2; 11:7, 17–18; 11:55) correspond to the three journeys to Jerusalem in Luke's central section (Luke 9:51; 13:22; 17:11).[6] The present writer follows this scheme with slight modifications.

The first of three journeys to Jerusalem (Luke 9:51–13:21; John 7:10–10:42) begins shortly after Jesus made His secret journey to Jerusalem for the Feast of Tabernacles (John 7:2, 10), after which He presumably returned to Galilee. From Galilee He started to make a journey to Jerusalem (Luke 9:51; John 10:22–39) to eventually attend the Feast of Dedication, December 18, AD 32.[7] The ministry between Galilee and Jerusalem was in Samaria (Luke 9:52–56) where He sent out the seventy (10:1–24) probably into the regions of Samaria and Perea. After their return Jesus had an extensive ministry (10:25–13:21), before arriving in Jerusalem for the Feast of the Dedication. This marks the end of the first of these final three journeys to Jerusalem.

After the feast, Jesus went to Perea (John 10:40–42). In preparing to return to Jerusalem (Luke 13:22) for His second journey, He had an extensive ministry of miracles and parables probably all in Perea (13:22–17:10). He finally went to Jerusalem to raise Lazarus (John 11:1–54, especially verses 7, 17–18). This marks the close of the second of the final three journeys to Jerusalem.

The third journey to Jerusalem is the final one. After raising Lazarus, Jesus went to Ephraim (11:54) and from there He possibly continued north to the borders of Samaria and Galilee. (See Luke 17:11, where Samaria is mentioned before Galilee.) From there, Jesus made His final journey to Jerusalem as is given in Luke 17:11–19:28 and is paralleled in Matthew 19:1–20:34 and Mark 10:1–52. In His final journey, His ministry of miracles and parables was probably accomplished primarily in Perea and Judea. Finally, Jesus went to Jerusalem for the Passover (John 11:55–12:1) and remained until His death in AD 33.[8]

. . . There will be those who disagree with the arrangement of the above itinerary, but to fit it into less than a three-and-a-half-year period seems highly unlikely. Jesus's ministry, then, began in the summer or autumn of AD 29 and came to an end at the Passover of AD 33.

How to *Begin* a Relationship with God

The life of Jesus was the most extraordinary and significant life in human history. No potentate, prince, or poet ever lived a more interesting and important life than did Jesus. Yet, He was born to peasant parents, labored in an obscure profession, and by the time of His death, had little more than a hundred people following His teaching. Jesus lived in a backwater province of the great Roman Empire, wrote no books, and accomplished His mission in a mere three and a half years. So why do we know more about His life than about the lives of various emperors who claimed the title of god?

Jesus not only claimed to be God, He proved that He was (and is) God. Only a holy God could live a sinless life. And no one has ever lived such a life but Jesus. This is but one proof of Jesus's deity. Others include His death and resurrection—and His power displayed in the lives of His followers for centuries. If you'd like to learn more about Jesus and how He can transform your life, keep reading. We begin with four essential truths.

Our Spiritual Condition: Totally Depraved

The first truth is rather personal. One look in the mirror of Scripture, and our human condition becomes painfully clear:

> "There is none righteous, not even one;
> There is none who understands,
> There is none who seeks for God;
> All have turned aside, together they have become useless;
> There is none who does good,
> There is not even one." (Romans 3:10–12)

We are all sinners through and through—totally depraved. Now, that doesn't mean we've committed every atrocity known to humankind. We're not as *bad* as we can be, just as *bad off* as we can be. Sin colors all our thoughts, motives, words, and actions.

If you've been around a while, you likely already believe it. Look around. Everything around us bears the smudge marks of our sinful nature. Despite our best efforts to create a perfect world, crime statistics continue to soar, divorce rates keep climbing, and families keep crumbling.

Something has gone terribly wrong in our society and in ourselves—something deadly. Contrary to how the world would repackage it, "me-first" living doesn't equal rugged individuality and freedom; it equals death. As Paul said in his letter to the Romans, "The wages of sin is death" (Romans 6:23)—our spiritual and physical death that comes from God's righteous judgment of our sin, along with all of the emotional and practical effects of this separation that we experience on a daily basis. This brings us to the second marker: God's character.

God's Character: Infinitely Holy

How can God judge us for a sinful state we were born into? Our total depravity is only half the answer. The other half is God's infinite holiness.

The fact that we know things are not as they should be points us to a standard of goodness beyond ourselves. Our sense of injustice in life on this side of eternity implies a perfect standard of justice beyond our reality. That standard and source is God Himself. And God's standard of holiness contrasts starkly with our sinful condition.

Scripture says that "God is Light, and in Him there is no darkness at all" (1 John 1:5). God is absolutely holy—which creates a problem for us. If He is so pure, how can we who are so impure relate to Him?

Perhaps we could try being better people, try to tilt the balance in favor of our good deeds, or seek out methods for self-improvement. Throughout history, people have attempted to live up to God's standard by keeping the Ten Commandments or living by their own code of ethics. Unfortunately, no one can come close to satisfying the demands of God's law. Romans 3:20 says, "By the works of the Law no flesh will be justified in His sight; for through the Law comes the knowledge of sin."

Our Need: A Substitute

So here we are, sinners by nature and sinners by choice, trying to pull ourselves up by our own bootstraps to attain a relationship with our holy Creator. But every time we try, we fall flat on our faces. We can't live a good enough life to make up for our sin, because God's standard isn't "good enough"—it's *perfection*. And we can't make amends for the offense our sin has created without dying for it.

Who can get us out of this mess?

If someone could live perfectly, honoring God's law, and would bear sin's death penalty for us—in our place—then we would be saved from our predicament. But is there such a person? Thankfully, yes!

Meet your substitute—*Jesus Christ*. He is the One who took death's place for you!

> [God] made [Jesus Christ] who knew no sin to be sin on our behalf, so that we might become the righteousness of God in Him. (2 Corinthians 5:21)

GOD'S PROVISION: A SAVIOR

God rescued us by sending His Son, Jesus, to die on the cross for our sins (1 John 4:9–10). Jesus was fully human and fully divine (John 1:1, 18), a truth that ensures His understanding of our weaknesses, His power to forgive, and His ability to bridge the gap between God and us (Romans 5:6–11). In short, we are "justified as a gift by His grace through the redemption which is in Christ Jesus" (Romans 3:24). Two words in this verse bear further explanation: *justified* and *redemption*.

Justification is God's act of mercy, in which He declares righteous the believing sinners while we are still in our sinning state. Justification doesn't mean that God *makes* us righteous, so that we never sin again, rather that He *declares* us righteous—much like a judge pardons a guilty criminal. Because Jesus took our sin upon Himself and suffered our judgment on the cross, God forgives our debt and proclaims us PARDONED.

Redemption is Christ's act of paying the complete price to release us from sin's bondage. God sent His Son to bear His wrath for all of our sins—past, present, and future (Romans 3:24–26; 2 Corinthians 5:21). In humble obedience, Christ willingly endured the shame of the cross for our sake (Mark 10:45; Romans 5:6–8; Philippians 2:8). Christ's death satisfied God's righteous demands. He no longer holds our sins against us, because His own Son paid the penalty for them. We are freed from the slave market of sin, never to be enslaved again!

PLACING YOUR FAITH IN CHRIST

These four truths describe how God has provided a way to Himself through Jesus Christ. Because the price has been paid in full by God, we must respond to His free gift of eternal life in total faith and confidence in Him to save us. We must step forward into the relationship with God that He has prepared for us—not by doing good works or by being a good person, but by coming to Him just as we are and accepting His justification and redemption by faith.

> For by grace you have been saved through faith; and that not of yourselves, it is the gift of God; not as a result of works, so that no one may boast. (Ephesians 2:8–9)

We accept God's gift of salvation simply by placing our faith in Christ alone for the forgiveness of our sins. Would you like to enter a relationship with your Creator by trusting in Christ as your Savior? If so, here's a simple prayer you can use to express your faith:

> *Dear God,*
>
> *I know that my sin has put a barrier between You and me. Thank You for sending Your Son, Jesus, to die in my place. I trust in Jesus alone to forgive my sins, and I accept His gift of eternal life. I ask Jesus to be my personal Savior and the Lord of my life. Thank You. In Jesus's name, amen.*

If you've prayed this prayer or one like it and you wish to find out more about knowing God and His plan for you in the Bible, contact us at Insight for Living Ministries. Our contact information is on the following page.

We Are Here *for You*

If you desire to find out more about knowing God and His plan for you in the Bible, contact us. Insight for Living Ministries provides staff pastors who are available for free written correspondence or phone consultation. These seminary-trained and seasoned counselors have years of experience and are well-qualified guides for your spiritual journey.

Please feel welcome to contact your regional Pastoral Ministries by using the information below:

United States
Insight for Living
Pastoral Ministries
Post Office Box 269000
Plano, Texas 75026-9000
USA
972-473-5097,
(Monday through Friday,
8:00 a.m. – 5:00 p.m. central time)
www.insight.org/contactapastor

Canada
Insight for Living Canada
Pastoral Ministries
PO Box 8 Stn A
Abbotsford BC   V2T 6Z4
CANADA
1-800-663-7639
info@insightforliving.ca

Australia, New Zealand, and South Pacific
Insight for Living Australia
Pastoral Care
Post Office Box 443
Boronia, VIC 3155
AUSTRALIA
1300 467 444

United Kingdom and Europe
Insight for Living United Kingdom
Pastoral Care
PO Box 553
Dorking
RH4 9EU
UNITED KINGDOM
0800 787 9364
+44 (0)1306 640156
pastoralcare@insightforliving.org.uk

Ordering *Information*

If you would like to order additional copies of *Three Years with Jesus: A Pictorial Journey Through the Ministry of Christ* or order other Insight for Living Ministries resources, please contact the office that serves you.

United States
Insight for Living
Post Office Box 269000
Plano, Texas 75026-9000
USA
1-800-772-8888
(Monday through Friday,
7:00 a.m. – 7:00 p.m. central time)
www.insight.org
www.insightworld.org

Canada
Insight for Living Canada
PO Box 8 Stn A
Abbotsford BC V2T 6Z4
CANADA
1-800-663-7639
www.insightforliving.ca

Australia, New Zealand, and South Pacific
Insight for Living Australia
Post Office Box 443
Boronia, VIC 3155
AUSTRALIA
1300 467 444
www.insight.asn.au

United Kingdom and Europe
Insight for Living United Kingdom
PO Box 553
Dorking
RH4 9EU
UNITED KINGDOM
0800 787 9364
www.insightforliving.org.uk

Other International Locations
International constituents may contact the U.S. office through our Web site (www.insightworld.org), mail queries, or by calling +1-972-473-5136.

Ruins on the southern end of the Temple Mount

$Questions$ FOR FAMILY TALKS AND GROUP DISCUSSIONS

OUT OF EGYPT, devotion on page 7

Matthew 2:13–16, 19–23

Jesus was born King of the Jews, but a rival sat on His throne threatening to kill the newborn King. Mary and Joseph escaped to Egypt to protect Jesus until it was safe to return.

1. Do you believe you were born for a specific purpose? If so, what? If not, why not?

2. Discuss a time you had to wait before accomplishing something truly significant in your life.

3. Why do you think God didn't just coronate Jesus as King over Israel immediately after His birth?

IN HIS FATHER'S HOUSE, devotion on page 9

Luke 2:41–52

It made perfect sense for God's Son to be in God's House, but Mary and Joseph didn't think about that as they frantically searched for the lost boy.

1. Read Luke 2:47–49. What do you think of Jesus's response to Mary's question?

2. What did Jesus do, and what was His attitude, according to Luke 2:51?

3. What do Jesus's answer, His action, and His attitude teach us about Him as a 12-year-old boy? How might you apply that to your life?

BAPTISM — A SYMBOLIC DOORWAY, devotion on page 13

Matthew 3

God the Son began His public ministry with a public commission by God the Father and a public confirmation by God the Spirit.

1. Why do you think Jesus submitted Himself to baptism by John?

2. How important is baptism to your spiritual life and to the spiritual life of the community of faith?

3. Have you been baptized? If so, discuss that decision and its significance to you. If not, discuss why.

FAITHFUL IN THE WILDERNESS, devotion on page 15

Matthew 4:1–11

We live in a world filled with temptations. Thankfully, we have a Savior who faced temptation too but didn't fall to its lure. As Hebrews 4:15 states, "We do not have a high priest who cannot sympathize with our weaknesses, but One who has been tempted in all things as we are, yet without sin."

1. Not all of us are tempted by the same things. What are some temptations you find difficult to resist?

2. The temptations Jesus faced from Satan covered the broad range of human desires: appetites to satisfy the body, enticements to satisfy the soul, and inducements to satisfy the ego. What did Jesus do to fend off each of these attacks?

3. What should you do to resist temptations that come into your life? What does this require of you?

CALLING SOME OF THE FIRST DISCIPLES, devotion on page 17

John 1:35–51

Discipleship is the high calling of becoming like Christ. There are many true followers of Jesus but few true disciples.

1. If Jesus walked the earth today and He were to say to you, "Come, follow Me," what would be your answer?

2. According to Matthew 16:24, what is the cost of discipleship?

3. What does denying yourself and taking up your cross look like for you?

WATER TO WINE, devotion on page 19

John 2:1–11

Jesus cares about our everyday concerns of life—not just about the "big" things, as this first of many miracles attests.

1. Why do you think Mary was so confident that Jesus would do something about the wine problem at the wedding?

2. Whether large or small, what concerns you today?

3. Do you think Jesus is concerned about what concerns you? If not, why not? If so, what should you do to seek a solution to your problem?

THE PURPOSE OF HIS MIRACLES, devotion on page 23

Matthew 11:20–23; John 20:30–31

Jesus was the miracle worker *par excellence*. Oh, He wasn't the only miracle worker of His day, but none surpassed Him in doing "signs and wonders." And while others performed miracles for selfish reasons, Jesus performed miracles for selfless reasons—so people might come to saving faith in Him.

1. The greatest miracle of all was the resurrection of Jesus. Do you believe Jesus died for your sins and was raised from the dead three days later? If so, what difference has that belief made in your life? If not, please read and discuss "How to Begin a Relationship with God" on page 62.

2. Many claim to work miracles today. What is the motivation of these modern-day "miracle" workers?

3. Name a couple of miracles that Jesus performed during His earthly ministry (flip through any of the Gospels to find them). What was the result of each?

JESUS'S NIGHT VISITOR, devotion on page 25

John 3:1–21

In what is one of the most well-known conversations in the Bible, Jesus confounded the Jewish scholar who would later become a faithful follower, Nicodemus.

1. What *didn't* Nicodemus understand about Jesus's claim that one must be born again?

2. All humans have been rendered bitten by sin. Jesus likened the account recorded in Numbers 21:4–9 to His own future crucifixion. What did people in Old Testament times have to do to be saved from the snakes, and what did Jesus tell Nicodemus he must do to be saved?

3. Jesus was sent into the world to save the world, not to judge it (John 3:16–17). So what did Jesus mean when He said that those who do not believe are judged already (3:18–21)?

A NEW KIND OF FISHING, devotion on page 27

Luke 5:1–11

When we come to grips with who Jesus really is, our lives are never the same. This was true of Peter and the other disciples who gave up their business as fishermen to become fishers of men.

1. Think about your life before you came to faith in Christ and your life afterward. How has your life changed?

2. Why would a large catch of fish cause Peter to fall at Jesus's feet and confess his sin?

3. When was the last time you had a moment like Peter's?

MERCY TO THE MISERABLE, devotion on page 29

John 5:1–18

Jesus was the Great Physician, who showed mercy to those in need of healing. He continues to heal those who are broken in body, in mind, and in spirit.

1. Describe a time in your life when you were broken physically, mentally, or spiritually and in need of divine mercy.

2. What did the Lord do for you during that time?

3. How might you help another person in need of mercy based on what you learned from your time of need?

THE LEADERS' BURDEN OF REST, devotion on page 33

Mark 2:23–28

The Pharisees turned a day of rest and holy celebration into a day of restlessness and unholy legalism. While the Pharisees lorded over the people with unbiblical rules about the Sabbath, Jesus declared He is Lord over the Sabbath.

1. Briefly describe the scene in Mark 2:23–26 and why the Pharisees were upset with Jesus.

2. What was Jesus's conclusion in Mark 2:27–28?

3. How might you apply this to your life of faith?

TELL ME A STORY, devotion on page 35

Matthew 13:1–23

Jesus was the master storyteller. And the stories He loved to tell were parables—pithy narratives of everyday activities intended to communicate spiritual truths.

1. What is your favorite parable? Why?

2. What does your favorite parable teach you about spiritual truth?

3. What stories do you read or teach to your children or grandchildren to help them learn and understand spiritual truths?

TRAINING THE TWELVE, devotion on page 37

John 6:1–13

Life is challenging. Of that there is no doubt. But it seems especially challenging when we believe we don't have sufficient provisions—whether it be food, money, time, or strength—to meet the difficulties of life. Thankfully, we have a Lord who specializes in multiplying what little provisions we have, if only we'd surrender them to Him.

1. Does the feeding of the five thousand seem too incredible to believe? Explain.

2. What have you faced in your life that you'd consider equivalent to feeding five thousand with a sack lunch? In other words, what impossibility have you faced in life?

3. What did you do to meet the impossibility? What did God do to meet the impossibility?

JESUS GIVES A POP QUIZ, devotion on page 39

Mark 6:45–52

We often miss the point of what God is trying to do in our lives. The disciples missed the point of the feeding of the five thousand—that Jesus was God and could care for all human needs. So Jesus demonstrated another feat that only God could do—walk on the water and control the weather.

1. Think about the impossibility you discussed earlier. What was the Lord trying to teach you through that experience?

2. What would you have thought if you were in the boat with the disciples and saw Jesus strolling along the surface of the lake?

3. What current need do you face that only the Lord can meet?

THINNING THE CROWD, devotion on page 41

John 6:24–71

Jesus rarely did or said what was expected. He was full of surprises, because the people who gathered around Him misunderstood His mission. And to many, He proved a disappointment when He didn't meet their expectations.

1. What do you expect of Jesus?

2. Describe a time when Jesus disappointed you.

3. Though Jesus didn't meet your expectations and disappointed you, can you still declare as Peter did: "Lord, to whom shall we go? You have words of eternal life" (John 6:68)?

BREAKING WITH TRADITION, devotion on page 45

Matthew 15

Traditions can enrich our spiritual lives. But traditions can turn into traditionalism, which will poison our spiritual lives. Jesus often encountered Pharisees and scribes who had become intoxicated on the poison of traditionalism and who passed on the destruction through their teaching.

1. What spiritual traditions do you practice in your personal and church life?

2. How biblically informed are the traditions of your personal and church life?

3. Have any of your traditions slipped into traditionalism, where the tradition has become more important than the truth of God's Word? If so, which ones, and what should you do about it?

JESUS HAS A QUESTION, devotion on page 47

Matthew 16:13–19

Jesus didn't run His ministry on opinion polls and focus groups, but on one significant day, Jesus wanted the opinions of the crowd. More important, He wanted the opinion of His disciples.

1. Why do you think Jesus asked the disciples about the opinions of the crowd?

2. What is significant about Peter's confession to the question, "Who do you say that I am?"

3. How would you answer Jesus's question? If it's something different than Peter's answer, consider reading "How to Begin a Relationship with God" on page 62.

A FIRST: JESUS TELLS OF HIS DEATH, devotion on page 49

Matthew 16:20–27

From the very beginning, Satan has sought to destroy God's plan to redeem sinful humanity. Satan tried to snuff out the life of the baby Jesus. During Jesus's ministry, Satan tried to divert Jesus from fulfilling His mission of giving His life as a sacrifice for us. And Satan would have used any means available to keep Jesus from the cross, even one of Jesus's own disciples.

1. Describe a time in your life when your own sinfulness distorted your testimony—your evidence of being a follower of Christ.

2. As you go throughout your daily life, what would you say is truer: that you have your mind set on God's interests or that you have your mind set on your interests?

3. If you want to increasingly set your mind on God's interests, what should you do?

A CONFIRMATION OF COMING GLORY, devotion on page 51

Matthew 16:24–17:8

Jesus's transfiguration on the mountain was an earthly manifestation of His heavenly glory as the Son of God. Though Peter was ready for Christ's kingdom to begin then and there, Moses and Elijah understood that Jesus must first endure suffering—a necessary truth for all who wish to follow Jesus into His kingdom.

1. What is required of all who wish to follow Jesus, according to Matthew 16:24–25?

2. What is your cross? What do you have to deny in order to follow Jesus?

3. God the Father announced His pleasure in His Son and commanded that we should listen to Jesus. What does it mean to listen to Jesus?

THE HEALING AT SILOAM, devotion on page 53

John 9

We live in a world lost in the darkness of perpetual blindness. Jesus healed a man who was blind because he was born into a sinful world. The blindness of the Pharisees was a result of their sin-filled hearts.

1. What did Jesus mean when He said He came "for judgment" (John 9:39)? (Hint: who are those who do not see but may and who are those who see and may become blind?)

2. What did Jesus mean when He said, "If you were blind, you would have no sin; but since you say, 'We see,' your sin remains" (9:41)?

3. How do these two statements relate to the healing of the blind man and to the blindness of the Pharisees?

THE RESURRECTION AND THE LIFE, devotion on page 55

John 11:1–46

Sin has the power to kill, but God has the power to give life. That's what Jesus did in the dead body of Lazarus—that's what Jesus will do for all who believe that He is the resurrection and the life.

1. If you were a member of Lazarus's family, what would you have thought and said when Jesus indicated that He would raise your dead brother to life?

2. Describe the feelings and thoughts you would have if you could embrace a departed loved one today.

3. What is the hope found in 1 Thessalonians 4:13–17?

THE GATHERING STORM, devotion on page 57

John 11:47–57

Jesus was a marked man. After Jesus raised Lazarus from the dead, the Pharisees could stomach no more. A plot to seize and kill Jesus began to form in their minds.

1. If you had been standing with Lazarus's family and friends and witnessed Lazarus walking out of the tomb, what would your reaction to Jesus have been?

2. What was the reaction of the crowd, according to John 11:45–46?

3. Why were the Pharisees so insistent on finding a way to kill Jesus?

THE ROAD UP TO JERUSALEM, devotion on page 59

Mark 10:32–34

Some roads in life lead to sorrow. Some roads in life lead to glory. The road to Jerusalem led to both—the sorrow of Jesus's crucifixion and the glory of His resurrection. The roads of our lives can also hold both—the sorrow of sin and its consequences but also the glory of forgiveness and life anew in Jesus, our wonderful Savior and Lord.

1. What are some of the consequences you've suffered as a result of sin in your life?

2. What is significant about Jesus's sacrificial death on the cross in regard to your sin?

3. What is significant about Jesus's glorious resurrection from the dead in regard to the consequences of your sin?

A portion of the "Ascent of Adummim," the road Jesus walked from Jericho up to Jerusalem

PREPARATIONS . . .

1. Adapted from Charles R. Swindoll, *Jesus: The Greatest Life of All* (Nashville: Thomas Nelson, 2008), 47.

2. Adapted from Swindoll, *Jesus*, 48–50.

THE EARLY MONTHS OF MINISTRY . . .

1. Adapted from Charles R. Swindoll, *Jesus: The Greatest Life of All* (Nashville: Thomas Nelson, 2008), 51–52.

2. Adapted from Swindoll, *Jesus*, 64–67.

3. Adapted from Swindoll, *Jesus*, 52–53.

4. Adapted from Swindoll, *Jesus*, 110–11.

5. Barton W. Johnson, *John: A Commentary for the People*, Accordance electronic ed. (1999), n.p.

A YEAR OF POPULARITY . . .

1. Adapted from Charles R. Swindoll, *Jesus: The Greatest Life of All* (Nashville: Thomas Nelson, 2008), 122–23.

2. Adapted from Swindoll, *Jesus*, 70–76.

3. Adapted from Swindoll, *Jesus*, 54–55, 261–62.

4. Adapted from Swindoll, *Jesus*, 113–15.

A YEAR OF TRANSITION . . .

1. Adapted from Charles R. Swindoll, *Jesus: The Greatest Life of All* (Nashville: Thomas Nelson, 2008), 80–82.

2. Alfred Edersheim, *The Life and Times of Jesus the Messiah*, Accordance electronic ed. (Altamonte Springs, Fla.: OakTree Software, 2006), n.p.

3. Adapted from Charles R. Swindoll, "Things That Strangle Us," in *The Finishing Touch: Becoming God's Masterpiece* (Dallas: Word, 1994), 126–28.

4. B. Cobbey Crisler, "The Acoustics and Crowd Capacity of Natural Theaters in Palestine," in *Biblical Archaeologist* (December 1976), 128–41.

5. Adapted from Swindoll, *Jesus*, 115–17.

6. Adapted from Swindoll, *Jesus*, 117–18.

7. Adapted from Swindoll, *Jesus*, 160–61.

THE FINAL YEAR: LOOKING AHEAD TO JERUSALEM . . .

1. Adapted from Charles R. Swindoll, *The Church Awakening: An Urgent Call for Renewal* (New York: FaithWords, 2010), 125–27.

2. Alfred Edersheim, *The Life and Times of Jesus the Messiah*, Accordance electronic ed. (Altamonte Springs, Fla.: OakTree Software, 2006), n.p..

3. Adapted from Charles R. Swindoll, "Jesus Has a Question for You," *Insights* (April 2007): 1–2.

4. Adapted from Swindoll, *The Church Awakening*, 40–41.

5. Adapted from Wayne Stiles, *Walking in the Footsteps of Jesus: A Journey Through the Lands and Lessons of Christ* (Ventura, Calif.: Regal Books, 2008), 88–89, 91.

6. Adapted from Charles R. Swindoll, *Jesus: The Greatest Life of All* (Nashville: Thomas Nelson, 2008), 118–20.

7. Adapted from Swindoll, *Jesus*, 120–22.

8. Adapted from Swindoll, *Jesus*, 141–42.

9. Adapted from Swindoll, *Jesus*, 157.

APPENDIX: OUTLINE OF CHRIST'S MINISTRY

This appendix is excerpted from Harold W. Hoehner, *Chronological Aspects of the Life of Christ* (Grand Rapids: Academic Books, © 1973, 1974, 1975 by Dallas Theological Seminary, © 1977 by Zondervan Corporation), 60–63.

1. Richard A. Parker and Waldo H. Dubberstein, *Babylonian Chronology 626 BC–AD 75*, 2nd ed. (Providence, R.I., 1956), 46.

2. Parker and Dubberstein, 46.

3. Parker and Dubberstein, 46.

4. For more discussion on this, see Harold W. Hoehner, *Herod Antipas* (Cambridge: Cambridge University Press, 1972), 317–30.

5. Parker and Dubberstein, 46.

6. Karl Wieseler, *Chronologische Synopse der vier Evangelium* (Hamburg: Perthes, 1843), 316–32.

7. Parker and Dubberstein, 46.

8. The evidence for this [is] discussed in chapter V [of Harold W. Hoehner, *Chronological Aspects of the Life of Christ* (Grand Rapids: Zondervan, 1977)].

Copyrights

Three Years with Jesus: A Pictorial Journey
Through the Ministry of Christ

From the Bible-Teaching Ministry of Charles R. Swindoll

Charles R. Swindoll has devoted his life to the clear, practical teaching and application of God's Word and His grace. A pastor at heart, Chuck has served as senior pastor to congregations in Texas, Massachusetts, and California. He currently serves as the senior pastor-teacher of Stonebriar Community Church in Frisco, Texas, but Chuck's listening audience extends far beyond a local church body. As a leading program in Christian broadcasting, *Insight for Living* airs in major Christian radio markets around the world, reaching people groups in languages they can understand. Chuck's extensive writing ministry has also served the body of Christ worldwide and his leadership as president and now chancellor of Dallas Theological Seminary has helped prepare and equip a new generation for ministry. Chuck and Cynthia, his partner in life and ministry, have four grown children and ten grandchildren.

Published By:

IFL Publishing House
A Division of Insight for Living
Post Office Box 251007, Plano, Texas 75025-1007

Editor in Chief: Cynthia Swindoll, President, Insight for Living
Executive Vice President: Wayne Stiles, Th.M., D.Min., Dallas Theological Seminary
General Editor: Wayne Stiles, Th.M., D.Min., Dallas Theological Seminary
Content Editor: Amy L. Snedaker, B.A., English, Rhodes College
Copy Editors: Jim Craft, M.A., English, Mississippi College
　　Kathryn Merritt, M.A., English, Hardin-Simmons University
Project Coordinator, Creative Ministries: Melanie Munnell, M.A., Humanities,
　　The University of Texas at Dallas
Project Coordinator, Publishing: Melissa Cleghorn, B.A., University of North Texas
Proofreader: Paula McCoy, B.A., English, Texas A&M University-Commerce

Art Director: Mike Beitler, B.F.A., Graphic Design, Abilene Christian University
Designer: Kari Pratt, B.A., Commercial Art, Southwestern Oklahoma State University
Images: Todd Bolen/BiblePlaces.com: front cover, pages 2, 4–5, 18, 20–21, 22, 23, 30–31, 34, 35, 36, 38, 39, 44, 52, 54, 58, 59, 70, back cover
　　Wayne Stiles: pages 23, 25, 26, 28, 39, 40, 41, 46, 47, 49, 51, 53, 57
　　Isam Siam: page 73
　　WikiMedia Commons Images:
　　　　Public Domain: pages 7, 10–11
　　　　Used pursuant to Creative Commons 1.0 Generic license:
　　　　　　Prokop Remeš: page 48
　　　　Used pursuant to Creative Commons Attribution 3.0:
　　　　　　High Contrast: page 16
　　　　Used pursuant to Creative Commons Attribution 3.0 Unported license:
　　　　　　Ariely: page 8
　　　　　　Michimaya: page 24
　　　　　　Sandstein: page 29
　　　　　　Bukvoed: page 59
　　　　Used pursuant to Creative Commons Attribution-Share Alike 2.5 Generic license:
　　　　　　Disdero: page 17
　　　　Used pursuant to Creative Commons Attribution-Share Alike 3.0 Unported license:
　　　　　　Nemo: page 29
　　　　　　Grauesel: page 37
　　　　　　Adiel lo: page 50
　　　　　　page 51: עקב׳
　　　　Used pursuant to Creative Commons CC0 1.0 Universal Public Domain license:
　　　　　　David Castor: page 55
　　　　Used pursuant to GNU Free Documentation Licenser version 1.2 or later:
　　　　　　Olaf Tausch: page 7
　　　　　　Koosg: page 9

ISBN: 978-1-57972-957-8
Printed in the United States of America